LEONARDO DA VINCI

Elizabeth Elias Kaufman

Galley Press

ISBN: 0-86136-067-2

CONTENTS

COLOR ILLUSTRATIONS

LEONARDO DA VINCI

Leonardo da Vinci was the personification of the Renaissance man: painter, architect, costume designer, author, botanist, musician, engineer, inventor, mathematician, all these and more. Today, he is remembered as the painter who created what has become the most well-known single piece of art in the world, the *Mona Lisa* (plate 38).

Although Leonardo's first works were created during the early Renaissance, most of his best work belongs to the period known as the High Renaissance. This was a short period that followed the earlier Renaissance. In order to better understand the artist and his work, it is always necessary to understand the age in which the artist lived. In Leonardo's case, it is best to begin with the Renaissance.

HIS TIMES

The Renaissance occurred during the fifteenth century. Although the word "renaissance" means rebirth, this century is also known as the Revival of Learning and as the Age of Discovery. It was a wondrous time in Europe. The shackles of the Middle Ages were finally removed, and men were free to explore again. This exploration took several forms, including the discovery of America, and the rediscovery of ancient art and culture.

The Renaissance began in Italy. There were several reasons for this. New ideas were filtering in through trade routes, most of which crossed Italy. The country went through tremendous changes in economy and politics. The Greeks and Romans had left Italy an enormous amount of classical art. All of these factors were important; however, the Renaissance developed largely as a result of a philosophical change in Italian thought.

During the Middle Ages, the Church dominated art and culture. The artist was a craftsman. His job was to illustrate religious scenes and ideas in a way that would help make them understandable to the masses. At the very end of the fourteenth century, there was a change in the relative importance of religious and secular matters. The Church began to lose its dominance. Christianity was still an important part of life, but new value was attached to material objects. No longer was life on earth thought of as only a stopping place in the march to eternal life. During the Renaissance, life on earth assumed added importance. Philosophers rediscovered classical philosophy and attempted to reconcile it with Christianity. This reconciliation meant that an artist was not simply a craftsman. He became a creator.

The Renaissance was characterized by three overlapping philosophies: classicism, humanism, and individualism. The rediscovery of classical Greek and Roman art and culture produced a profusion of nudes. No nudes had been used during the Middle Ages. The humanism of the Renaissance involved a translation of religious themes into natural instead of symbolic terms. Abstractions were illustrated as they impacted on man. The large number of famous Renaissance artists is proof of the importance of individualism during this period. Instead of simply illustrating religious themes, the Renaissance artist used his own ideas and concepts. The artist had the freedom to interpret the world around him.

The High Renaissance occurred during a relatively brief span of time at the end of the fifteenth century and beginning of the sixteenth century. There were only a few real masters: Bramante, Leonardo da Vinci, Michelangelo, Raphael, Titian and Giorgionne. There were even fewer minor artists. So overpowering was the art these men created, it was almost three hundred years before art scholars and the general public "rediscovered" the art that had been produced during the early Renaissance.

The period of the High Renaissance is often thought of as the climax or logical conclusion to the Renaissance. In many respects, this is true. The art created during this period was a reaction to the excesses of the earlier Renaissance. The philosophic characteristics of the earlier period: classicism, humanism, and individualism were all part of the High Renaissance. However, each of the characteristics underwent a change.

The superficiality that had pervaded early Renaissance humanism gave way to more idealized forms during the High Renaissance. The artist attempted to use ideas and ideals that had universal meaning and appeal. Thus, the young girl Madonna of the earlier Renaissance became a woman during the High Renaissance, capable of a woman's joys and sorrows. By introducing tension and strain to his art, the artist moved away from the generalization that was so much a part of classi-

cism. Perhaps the most significant change involved the concept of individualism. During the High Renaissance, the artist was viewed as a genius whose skills and inspiration had a "divine" origin. This Neoplatonic philosophy had two important consequences. It encouraged artists to undertake large and complicated projects, and it prodded wealthy men to support the artist and to commission his works.

The art of the High Renaissance is identified by several characteristics. Works created during this period are often very large. The *Last Supper* (plate 24) is thirty feet long and fourteen feet high. The idealized type is in some ways similar to Greek art. In contrast to Greek art, however, there is strain and tension in High Renaissance art. The final artistic characteristic of the High Renaissance, a sense of drama, is perhaps the most striking. It is the drama, the visual excitement, that seems to elevate the art of this period. There is nothing soothing about High Renaissance art. It demands the active participation of the viewer.

This was a period of drastic change. For the first time artists used their intellect as well as their artistic skills. There were changes in the basic composition of art works. Geometry was used to develop greater plasticity. Fifteenth century discoveries such as anatomy and perspective were incorporated as part of art, used to help enhance the art instead of displayed as a new toy.

Given the prevailing philosophy, it isn't surprising that the High Renaissance lasted for such a brief span of time. Each of the masters was a genius. Although their techniques could be taught to gifted followers, the spark that defines genius could not be transmitted. When the masters died, the High Renaissance ended. But in this short period, they created some of the finest art works of all time.

HIS LIFE

Leonardo da Vinci was born on April 15, 1452 in Vinci, a small town in Tuscany ("da Vinci" means of Vinci). He was the illegitimate son of Piero da Vinci, a fairly well-to-do notary. Of his mother, almost nothing is known except that her name was Caterina. It is assumed that she was a peasant.

Illegitimacy carried little social stigma in Leonardo's day. In fact, a few years after he was born, he was adopted by his natural father. Leonardo moved in with the man and his family and was treated as a legitimate son. Very little is known of his childhood.

Like most young men, Leonardo's schooling included reading, writing, mathematics, and a smattering of Latin. He was to remain fascinated by mathematics all his life. Latin was always a problem for him. Much has been made of Leonardo's handwriting. It cannot be read properly without using a mirror. Whether his backwards style was an attempt at secrecy or simply an easy way for a left-handed person to write is not known.

Leonardo is described as having great physical beauty, strength, and charm. A talented musician and singer, he was also an excellent conversationalist. Strangely, this talented man preferred his own company to the company of others. In his many notebooks, there is only one personal detail: a one-sentence factual notation of his father's death. Although the notebooks record many facets of his life, there is no indication of his inner feelings. The "personification of the Renaissance man" was truly a private individual.

When Leonardo was approximately fifteen, his father, recognizing the boy's talents, arranged for him to become an apprentice in the workshop of Andrea del Verrocchio, one of the leading artists in Italy.

Verrocchio had many different types of commissions. He was a painter and sculptor, but he also worked with jewelry, designed costumes, and created mosaics. Leonardo learned something of each of these arts by working on the details. Among the first commissions he worked on was the copper ball and cross that was placed on the dome of a cathedral. Leonardo served the customary six year apprenticeship and in 1472, at the age of twenty, he was admitted to the painter's guild. For the next four years or so, he continued to work in Verrocchio's studio.

During this time, he assisted Verrocchio in painting part of the *Baptism of Christ* (plate 1). The part worked on by Leonardo stands out like a sore thumb. The angel on the extreme left (plate 2) was definitely his work and not Verrocchio's. According to a story popular at the time, when Verrocchio saw the work Leonardo had done on the *Baptism of Christ,* the master put down his brush and never painted again, so awed was he by his pupil's skill.

In 1496, Leonardo and three other young men were accused of homosexual acts committed against a fifth young man. The charge had been made anonymously. Leonardo was acquitted, but the effect of this trauma is not known.

Leonardo set up his own workshop in 1477 or 1478. Among the works executed in the next five years were *St. Jerome* (plate 15), which he never finished, and the *Benois Madonna* (plates 9, 10).

In 1482, he left Florence to work for the Duke of Milan. The *Adoration of the Magi* (plate 13) which had been commissioned by a monastery near Florence was never finished. The Duke hired him as a result of a letter Leonardo had written listing his abilities. It is interesting to note that of the ten qualifications Leonardo included, only the tenth concerns his art. The first nine refer to his engineering abilities.

From 1483 until 1499, Leonardo lived in Milan. Among the works created in Milan were several portraits, a model for a gigantic horse, costume designs for festivals and celebrations, and theatrical scenery. His most famous piece from this period is the *Last Supper* (plate 24) begun in 1495. This was commissioned for the large wall in the refectory of the Dominican monastery of Santa Maria delle Grazie.

In 1499, the French army entered Milan. Leonardo fled to Mantua at the invitation of Isabella d'Este. He was to have painted her portrait, but had only managed to finish a preliminary drawing before he returned to Florence in 1500.

In Florence, Leonardo worked on mathematics, studies of birds, and other scientific fields. For a while he worked for Cesare Borgia as a military engineer. His best known piece, the *Mona Lisa* (plate 38) was painted during this stay in Florence. He also accepted a commission to do a large wall painting for the city of Florence, to be called the *Battle of Anghiari.* The painting was never completed and was thought to have been destroyed. (As this book goes to press, art scholars are investigating the possibility that the *Battle of Anghiari* was not destroyed, but rather painted over by another artist and still exists under the second painting.) It is known only from copies of it made by other artists at the time. In 1504, Leonardo was appointed to a committee of approximately thirty artists asked to choose the location for Michelangelo's *David.*

Leonardo returned to Milan in 1506 at the request of Charles d'Ambroise, the French governor, to act as a technical advisor during the war against Venice. In addition to his military work, he designed and organized festivals. Continuing his own studies, he produced a large treatise on anatomy at this time. Although he continued to create, his productivity in painting slowed down.

From 1513 until 1516, Leonardo lived in Rome. He received no commissions while in Rome, but continued to work on his notebooks.

In 1517, along with his servant, Leonardo went to France to live in Ambroise. He was given a house and a pension. In 1519, at the age of sixty-seven Leonardo died. He was buried in Ambroise.

His thousands of pages of notebooks reveal all sorts of inventions. At one point, he planned to divert the course of a river for military purposes. The notebooks also indicate his goals in painting: to create an illusion of three dimensions where only two exist, and to illustrate the soul through the motions of the body.

Leonardo remains as much a mystery as the smile on his *Mona Lisa* (plate 38). A man who seemingly had every gift God can bestow on a man, was lonely all his life. Despite his extraordinary artistic talents, he was not especially prolific. Many of his works remained unfinished. It is almost as if his mind worked too quickly to stay very long on any one subject. Once the "problem" was solved, he moved on to other things. The majority of his paintings were created early in his life. As he grew older, he seemed to be interested in other, more scientific "problems". Perhaps in his later life, he felt he had solved every artistic "problem".

HIS WORKS

PLATES 1, 2

The angel on the left in Verrocchio's *Baptism of Christ* was painted by Leonardo. It is thought to be the first full figure Leonardo was allowed to paint for Verrocchio. The background above the two angels and the tuft of grass in front of them are also by Leonardo. His work on this painting provides a tremendous contrast with the harshness of the rest of the piece.

Verrocchio's bored angel takes no part in the proceedings. He doesn't seem to belong with the group of figures. In contrast, Leonardo's graceful angel (plate 2) is watching the action of the scene with rapt attention. His soft curly hair (notice the blue ribbon at the back of his head), faintly feminine face, and trace of a smile present the viewer with Leonardo's first attempt at idealized beauty. The angel's pose is indicative of motion. The body is turned in one direction, the face in another, adding strain to the figure. The folds of the drapery have been carefully detailed. Leonardo's angel appears to be the only real figure in the painting. Verrocchio's figures look like stick men compared with Leonardo's angel.

The background above the two angels shows the same concern for landscape detail that became an integral part of many of Leonardo's later works. The misty interplay of light and shadow created by Leonardo stands out from the rest of the background painted by Verrocchio. In fact, the story goes that after Verrocchio saw the work Leonardo did on the *Baptism of Christ*, Verrocchio never painted again.

PLATES 3, 4

The *Annunciation* was commissioned for the Convent of Monte Oliveto. Art scholars have argued about how much of it was actually done by Leonardo. Many scholars, however, feel that this could have been Leonardo's first commission. There is no doubt that the angel (plate 3) is at least partially his work; a drawing by his hand shows the angel's sleeve.

The scene shows the Lord's angel announcing to Mary (plate 4) that she will become the mother of Christ. Though this work belongs more to the early Renaissance than to the High Renaissance, there is a quiet charm and tenderness in the painting. Mary and the angel have both raised their hands in silent communication.

Both the carpet of flowers on which the angel kneels and the treatment of the trees in the background reveal Leonardo's love of nature and his interest in botany.

At one point, another artist enlarged the angel's wings. These were originally modeled on the wings of a bird and were more graceful.

PLATE 5

The portrait of *Ginevra de' Benci* is the subject of controversy among art scholars. One group insists that this couldn't possibly be Leonardo's work; another insists that his hand is obvious. Both sides make impressive points.

Those who believe *Ginevra de' Benci* to be Leonardo's work point to the background. Behind the juniper tree (in Italian, "ginevra" means juniper tree), the artist painted a reflecting pond and hinted at a city's skyline. Everything beyond the tree is wrapped in a mist, similar to the background in many of Leonardo's later works. The detail of the tree itself shows the artist's usual attention to nature.

However, according to those who feel that this is not Leonardo's work, the face is too flat and her hair too harsh. The light that strikes her hair is too hard and doesn't exhibit Leonardo's usual diffusion of light.

PLATE 6

This drawing, *Study of Drapery for Kneeling Figure*, reveals Leonardo's concern with drapery. He did many drawings of this sort. This one was probably for either a Madonna or an Annunciation. Notice that he has drawn the head in two different positions.

PLATES 7, 8

The painting known as the *Madonna with Carnation* (also called the *Virgin with Flowers* and the *Munich Madonna*) is another work about which art scholars differ. It is one of a group of three paintings (the others are the *Madonna di Piazza* and the *Dreyfus Madonna*) which are very similar. It is thought that either the same model was used or that they were modeled after each other.

While many critics claim that this is not Leonardo da Vinci's work, one of his drawings shows some of the same features that are used in the Virgin's face. The hair style, left hand of the Madonna, the drapery, background, and the use of chiaroscuro all seem to be Leonardo's work. However, the painting has seriously deteriorated. Evidence of an improper restoration is clear in the leathery quality of the painting, especially obvious on the Madonna's face.

PLATES 9, 10

Another one of Leonardo's early works, the *Benois Madonna,* shows the beginnings of his evolution into a master painter. Although the piece has been heavily overpainted, the idealized (yet very human) faces of the Madonna (plate 9) and the chubby Infant (plate 10) hold promise of his later works. The Madonna's delighted smile and the concentration of the Christ Child give the painting a very natural quality. At the same time, the halos remind the viewer that this is no ordinary mother and child.

The painting suffered severe damage when it was transferred from a wooden panel to a canvas.

PLATES 11, 12

The *Litta Madonna* (plate 12) takes its name from one of its owners, Count Litta of Milan. Art scholars are divided on whether or not it was painted by Leonardo. There are quite a few theories as to its source. Even dating it is a problem. Depending on which theory is accepted, it was begun in 1480 or in 1485.

The drawing (plate 11) is definitely Leonardo's work. One theory states that Leonardo started the painting, but that another artist finished it. The tilt of the Madonna's head and the resemblance to the drawing indicate that Leonardo was responsible for that portion of the painting. However, the Christ Child doesn't bear much resemblance to other children he painted.

The *Litta Madonna* is in poor condition as a result of two overpaintings.

PLATES 13, 14

The *Adoration of the Magi* is usually thought of as Leonardo's first major work. It was never finished. He had only completed the underpainting when he abandoned it. What he has left the viewer is an underpainting that is a monochrome of gold and brown with chiaroscuro.

The painting was commissioned by the monks of the convent of San Donato a Scopeto. It was to be their altarpiece. As always, Leonardo spent a great deal of time working on drawings and detailed sketches before he started painting. The preliminary drawings show how he worked on the perspective and geometry of the piece. In fact, this tortured planning and detail work may have exhausted his interest in the project. Although it is incomplete, it is a masterpiece.

Leonardo established new standards in two different areas with his *Adoration of the Magi.* Before this, the scene was set with the Virgin at a window or sitting on a throne. Leonardo chose to seat her outside, on a hill. This allowed him to show many more figures and details.

Also new was his psychological treatment of the subject matter. Leonardo dismissed the idea of a narrative and tried instead to portray the multitude of emotional reactions to the birth of the Christ Child. It is estimated that there are sixty figures in the painting. Each shows a different psychological reaction. The figures have been drawn with tremendous force and intensity. There is a vital sense of drama in this highly organized work.

Leonardo was the acknowledged master of the use of chiaroscuro, the interplay of light and darkness. Unfinished as it is, the *Adoration of the Magi* perfectly illustrates his use of this technique. Notice how softly the figures on the right are drawn. They never quite emerge from the background. His use of chiaroscuro emphasizes the main characters while using the subordinate characters to help develop his emotional tone.

The background of the *Adoration of the Magi* is very complicated and demonstrates Leonardo's varied skills. To the right, he has drawn warriors astride horses in the middle of what appears to be a pitched battle. To the left there is an architectural ruin. What could be ancient Greek or Roman statues are placed in front of the steps. A nude youth sits on one. These ruins contain an intricate series of intersecting arches.

The central part of the work containing the Virgin and Child and the kings is the least finished part of the picture. Nevertheless, we can see that the Virgin represents the beginning of the "Leonardo type".

In his preliminary work, Leonardo obviously spent a great deal of time working on the geometry of the piece. The dominant figures form a pyramid that starts with the Virgin's head. Above the Virgin, Leonardo uses an arch to encompass many of his figures.

PLATE 15

St. Jerome was painted before Leonardo left Florence for Milan. Like the *Adoration of the Magi* (plate 13), it is unfinished. Also like the *Adoration of the Magi,* the work shows intense emotion.

In his right hand, the saint holds a stone he is using to beat his breast. Notice that the lion is not threatening St. Jerome; rather, he seems to share the saint's passion. Leonardo has done a great deal of detailed anatomical work to give the figure its old and withered look.

The piece, painted on a wooden panel, has an interesting history. At one time it was cut into two pieces. The smaller piece on which the head had been painted was found in a cobbler's shop being used as a tabletop.

PLATES, 16, 17

Soon after he arrived in Milan, Leonardo painted *The Lady with the Ermine.* It is a portrait of Cecilia Gallerani at about age seventeen. She was the mistress of the Duke of Milan. The artist might have posed her with the ermine because it was one of the Duke's emblems.

Leonardo took great care with the details of the portrait. Layers of paint were used to help define her sensitive face. The ermine (plate 17), a member of the mink family, has been painted with full musculature. Every hair is shown, even the thin whiskers. Notice how the ermine's white hair picks up the reflected color where it comes in contact with the woman's costume.

The portrait was executed in the shape of a pyramid. The woman's head forms the top; her shoulders and arms represent the sides; her right forearm is the bottom. Leonardo also used circles and lines in this composition. The woman's beads and her hair frame her face in circles. The ribbons across her forehead help to accentuate her face.

The painting has not been well preserved. Several parts of it have been repainted. Among the most obvious places is the background. Leonardo's customary misty background has been painted over with black, and an inscription has been added in the upper left-hand corner.

PLATES 18, 19

This is the first version of a painting Leonardo executed twice. The second **Madonna of the Rocks** (plates 41, 42) was painted ten to fifteen years after this one. The painting was to be an altarpiece commissioned for the Church of the Immaculate Conception in Milan.

Leonardo has given the Madonna a very spiritual quality. Her face represents the famous "Leonardo type", except around the eyes. His use of chiaroscuro (light and darkness) is extraordinary. Notice the shaft of light that strikes the head of the Virgin and illuminates a small part of her costume. Light from a different source strikes the fingertips of her foreshortened left arm and hand.

The little St. John and the Christ Child are two chubby and sweet children. The angel on the right looks out at the viewer and points towards the scene. The finger is actually pointing at St. John, causing the eye to move from the pointing finger to St. John, to the Madonna, and then to the Christ Child.

The artist has created an incredible conjunction of hands in this **Madonna of the Rocks.** Hands painted by Leonardo always show great sensitivity. Here, the Madonna's hand protects the Christ Child; the angel's hand points towards St. John; St. John's hands are in a position of worship; and the Christ Child's hand blesses St. John.

The background and foreground are an interesting combination. The barren, almost forbidding rock formation recedes into the mist. In the foreground, Leonardo displays his scientific knowledge with flowers and stratified rocks.

This piece represents a transitional period for Leonardo. There is a great deal in this painting of the early Renaissance, but it is obvious that the artist has gone one step beyond. In fact, his next major piece, the **Last Supper** (plate 24) was one of the first High Renaissance pieces produced.

The **Madonna of the Rocks** was damaged when it was transferred from its wooden panel to canvas. It was retouched in several places. Additionally, the varnish has yellowed with time, distorting the colors.

PLATE 20

The painting known as the **Portrait of a Woman** shows a member of the Milanese Court. The woman's lovely jewelry is one of the many reasons art scholars question whether this is Leonardo's work. Most of his portraits use a minimum of jewelry. It is probable that if it is not Leonardo's work, it was painted in his workshop.

One of the details that would lend credence to the theory that this is Leonardo's work is the profusion of knots. Notice for example, the one on the sleeve of the angel in the **Annunciation** (plate 3) and on the shoulders of **La Belle Ferronnière** (plate 21).

PLATE 21

La Belle Ferronnière may or may not be Leonardo's work. Some feel that the entire portrait is too heavy to be the master's. It is true that the pose is stiff and unlike Leonardo's more natural posing. Additionally, the woman's features are thicker than those usually found in Leonardo's female portraits. However, the cords around her neck and the knotted ribbons on her shoulders do resemble Leonardo's style.

PLATE 22

The drawing of the **Girl with Bonnet** has obviously been altered. Some of the changes were probably made by Leonardo. However, the chin does not appear to be the work of Leonardo.

PLATE 23

This drawing of Christ, **The Savior,** was a study for the head of Christ in the **Last Supper** (plates 24, 25). It gives an indication of the amount of work that went into the planning for the painting. There were numerous such individual studies for each of the thirteen figures that appear in the **Last Supper.** This one is not in good condition. It has been overpainted several times.

PLATES 24, 25, 26, 27, 28, 29

The *Last Supper* is usually considered to be the first painting of the High Renaissance. All of the artistic characteristics of the High Renaissance are present in it. This is a monumental work. The painting occupies an entire upper wall that measures fourteen feet by thirty feet. The figures are half again as large as life. The work is intellectual and full of strain and tension. Christ's face has been idealized. Finally, it is a masterpiece of drama.

The work was commissioned by the Duke of Milan for the Dominican monks of the Church of Santa Maria delle Grazie in Milan. It was painted on their refectory wall. The painting almost seems to be an extension of the refectory itself. Despite the fact that it was immediately recognized as a masterpiece, it has been treated with something less than devotion. At one point, after the painting had seriously deteriorated, a door was cut through the wall, extending through the lower middle of the painting. The effects of this are still visible across the bottom of the painted tablecloth and downwards at Christ's place.

The subject of the painting, Christ's last Passover meal with his disciples, had been painted many times before. The figure of Judas had usually been shown on the near side of the table, physically separated from the twelve other figures. This placement, however, draws attention away from the focus of the scene, Christ. It also pinpoints the time, for it is obvious to all the participants who the traitor is. Leonardo arrived at a unique method of dealing with Judas. He was placed on the far side of the table with the other diners. The intellectual problem of handling thirteen figures on the same side of the table was solved with Leonardo's usual genius.

Christ has been placed in the middle of the table. His strong, calm, pyramid shape (plate 25) contrasts vividly with the agitation of the apostles. Leonardo focuses attention on Christ in several other ways. The largest of the three windows behind His head acts as a halo. The actions of the disciples also draw attention to Christ. Finally, the central vanishing point is just above Christ's head.

Leonardo has pictured the figures in the dramatically charged moment immediately after Christ announced, "One of you shall betray me." The psychological impact of the statement is obvious in the faces and gestures of each apostle. In contrast, Christ is perfectly calm. In fact, Leonardo has posed Christ so that the painting represents not only the moment shown; but also the Eucharist, for Christ's gesture shows His sacrifice.

Leonardo spent hours in the streets searching for models for the figures in the *Last Supper.* Although the face of Christ was the last face to be painted, he seemed to have the most trouble finding a model for Judas. He finally painted Judas in profile (plate 26), dark and glowering, recoiling from Christ.

The apostles are arranged in four groups of three figures. Closest to Christ are Thomas, James the Greater, and Phillip (plate 27). The head closest to Christ is Thomas's. His position indicates why he is known as "doubting Thomas". With outstretched arms, James the Greater seems to deny that such a thing could happen. Phillip's face and hands show his promise that he is not the one. On the other side of Christ, Peter is talking to John as Judas draws away (plate 26). On the extreme left, Andrew raises his hands; James the Lesser points; and Bartholomew rises (plate 28). Finally, to the extreme right, Matthew extends his arms towards Christ; but looks towards Thaddeus who is conversing with Simon (plate 29).

The *Last Supper* started to deteriorate soon after Leonardo finished painting it. Dissatisfied with fresco, he used an experimental method involving oil, tempera, and a new mixture as a base. The experiment failed; and the dampness in the room accelerated the deterioration. The painting was restored many times by incompetent artists. As mentioned earlier, a door was cut through part of the painting. During World War II, the building housing the *Last Supper* was bombed. The painting had been protected by sandbags; but the fact that it survived the bombing is a miracle. Finally, in 1946, Mauro Pellicioli, a master restorer, began to work on the painting. He removed much of the paint applied by earlier restorers and reattached the original flaking paint with a special treatment. When the job was completed in 1954, he had accomplished an almost perfect restoration.

PLATES 30, 31, 32, 33, 34, 35

The *Burlington House Cartoon* (also called the *St. Anne and the Virgin Cartoon)* takes its name from a gallery that once owned it. The work represents an early stage in Leonardo's preoccupation with the theme of the Virgin and Child with St. Anne. Despite its preliminary nature, many scholars feel that the *Burlington House Cartoon* is one of Leonardo's most impressive works. For many, it is a much finer piece than his *Virgin and Child with St. Anne* (plates 44, 45), which was the final stage in the theme.

In contrast with many of his other works, the geometry of this composition is primarily vertical. The pyramid shape, although present, does not totally dominate the piece. The Virgin is seated on her mother's lap, holding her son, who in turn is blessing St. John (plate 31). The animation evidenced by the expression of each figure gives life to the entire work.

By tradition, the Virgin was to be pictured in St. Anne's lap. The problems created by this are monumental. Leonardo solved them by concentrating attention on the interplay between the characters.

His use of chiaroscuro in the *Burlington House Cartoon* is exceptional. The mystery of St. Anne's face (plate 32), her strange smile, and deep, dark eyes are beautifully contrasted with the innocent and tender face of the Virgin (plate 33). The psychological drama of the Virgin's mother (who appears to be almost the same age as the Virgin) contemplating her daughter is accentuated by the careful use of chiaroscuro.

The gesture St. Anne makes with her left hand is a familiar one in Leonardo's work. It can be found in the first version of the *Madonna of the Rocks* (plate 18), in *St. John the Baptist* (plate 46), in *Bacchus* (plate 47), and in several other works.

The preliminary drawing of *St. Anne* (plate 34) has been retouched by another artist. Notice that in the cartoon, St. Anne's head is tilted to the left and not to the right as in this drawing. The drawing of the *Christ Child* (plate 35) was changed slightly in the cartoon. The eyes are more open and dominant in the drawing than in the cartoon.

PLATE 36

This *Study of Drapery* was done at about the same time Leonardo was working on the *Burlington House Cartoon* (plate 30). However, it was not used in it. Notice the similarity of the study and the unfinished legs of the Virgin in *Virgin and Child with St. Anne* (plate 44).

PLATE 37

Isabella d'Este was a great admirer of Leonardo. When he fled to Mantua, he stayed with her and began her portrait. The drawing pictured here has been retouched by another artist. Leonardo was in the process of transferring the drawing to a painting when he left Mantua. The portrait was never completed.

PLATES 38, 39

The *Mona Lisa* is the most famous portrait ever created. Her timeless expression and steady gaze have always fascinated viewers.

Mona Lisa is a portrait of Lisa Gherardini, the wife of Francesco del Giocondo, a nobleman living in Florence. Not much is known about this woman. One story has it that she lost her only child shortly before the work began. To lighten her mood, Leonardo is supposed to have had music played while she sat for him. It took Leonardo four years to paint this piece.

A psychological study of the personality portrayed in the *Mona Lisa* would require several volumes. Her smile has become synonymous with mystery. She is smiling with only the left part of her mouth as was the custom of the day. However, Leonardo has given her face both individual characteristics and an idealized form. Her face is the perfect example of the "Leonardo type" female face.

She has no jewelry or ornaments, unusual for the portrait of a noblewoman. Leonardo has not used these props in order to concentrate attention on the face and figure of the subject. She wears only a gossamer-thin veil over her hair. Her soft hands are relaxed and expressive. The artist has placed her against a background of rocks, winding paths, and pools of water. This is perhaps his best and most complete background. Unfortunately, the colors have changed and darkened. The paints Leonardo was experimenting with proved to be unstable.

Mona Lisa was not a commissioned work. When Leonardo left Italy to live in France, he took the portrait with him and sold it there. It was eventually hung in the Louvre. In August of 1911, an Italian stole it from the museum. It was missing for two years until, in 1913, the thief attempted to sell it to a dealer in Florence. He was arrested and the painting was returned to the Louvre.

PLATE 40

The *Portrait of a Young Lady* was painted during the early sixteenth century. Usually it is attributed to the studio of Leonardo, but not to Leonardo himself. The face does not conform to the "Leonardo type", and the misshapen body could not have been executed by Leonardo. The artist has shown the head in profile, while the body appears to be turned more towards the viewer. Because the neck and shoulders don't reflect this turning, the whole body appears to be out of proportion and distorted.

PLATES 41, 42

This *Madonna of the Rocks* is the second and last version of the painting. In the ten or fifteen years between the two versions, Leonardo's style changed from that of the early Renaissance to the High Renaissance. In order to illustrate the difference, several changes will be noted.

In the first version of *Madonna of the Rocks* (plates 18, 19), the angel on the right is pointing and looking towards the viewer. In the second version, the angel's gesture has been dropped and his gaze is towards the action of the scene, making him more a part of the grouping. In this second version, Leonardo has added halos and given St. John a cross. The artist has also changed St. John's pose to make it more natural. The drapery in the first version is heavy; in the second, it is more natural, less leaden. In the second version, Mary's left hand is less claw-like. Finally, the Madonna in the second painting is much larger than in the first. All of these changes combine to heighten the drama and tension in the second painting.

PLATE 43

The drawing, *Study for Leda*, is one of a number of drawings Leonardo made in preparation for a painting. Although the painting has been lost, the drawings give us a hint what it might have looked like.

PLATES 44, 45

The *Virgin and Child with St. Anne* represents one of the last works Leonardo executed involving the theme of these three figures. Its unfinished state is especially obvious in the Madonna's outer garment.

Unlike the *Burlington House Cartoon* (plate 30), on the same theme, this piece is very definitely based on a pyramid.

Many scholars prefer the *Burlington House Cartoon* to this painting. The face of the Madonna in the cartoon is much more natural than in the *Virgin and Child with St. Anne*. Here, her face has a wooden quality. The face of St. Anne in this painting is given more prominence. Leonardo has given her a wise, indulgent expression.

PLATE 46

Despite the brilliant use of chiaroscuro, the painting of *St. John the Baptist* is not nearly as effective as some of the artist's earlier works. It is an apparent attempt to focus attention on the saint and his cross. By eliminating his customary treatment of the background, Leonardo tried to emphasize the spiritual nature of the subject matter.

However, the face has a decidedly female quality that disturbs many viewers. The pointed finger is a gesture the artist used to better advantage in other paintings. Finally, the smile is more of a simper than a spiritually charged emotion.

PLATE 47

Bacchus was originally called *St. John the Baptist in the Desert.* The painting was later altered by the addition of an animal skin across the figure's lap, a leafy wreath in the hair, and by the removal of a bar from the cross, leaving a staff.

There are serious doubts as to the source of the painting. For many scholars, this is almost a caricature of a Leonardo painting. The figure has the familiar pointed finger on the right hand. An examination of the left hand reveals another pointed finger. The hands are soft, chubby, and not well formed. The landscape draws attention to itself instead of enhancing the subject. Finally, the foreground and immediate background are much too lush to be a desert.

PLATE 48

No book on Leonardo would be complete without an example of Leonardo's inventions in the field of military weapons. This one is known as *Explosive Bombardment.* The mortar explodes a bag containing explosive projectiles of different sizes. The projectiles are filled with gunpowder and pocked with holes so that they will explode on impact.

Plate 1 Verrocchio with Leonardo, **Baptism of Christ**, 1470-73,
tempera and oil on panel, 5′ 9⅝″ x 4′ 11½″, Uffizi, Florence

17

Plate 2 Verrocchio with Leonardo, **Baptism of Christ,**
detail - Leonardo's angel

Plate 3 Annunciation, detail - angel, c. 1472, oil on panel, Uffizi, Florence   19

Plate 4 Annunciation, detail - the Virgin

Plate 5 Ginevra de' Benci, 1474-78, 15 ⅛' x 14½",
National Gallery of Art, Washington, D.C.   21

Plate 6 Study of Drapery for Kneeling Figure, c. 1478, silverpoint, ink, and white on brown paper, 10⅛″ x 7¾″, National Print Room, Rome

Plate 7 Madonna with Carnation, detail - Madonna, c. 1478,
oil on panel, Altere Pinakothek, Munich

23

Plate 8 Madonna with Carnation, detail - Infant

Plate 9 Benois Madonna, detail - head of Madonna, 1478-80,
oil on canvas, Hermitage, Leningrad

Plate 10 Benois Madonna, detail - head of Infant

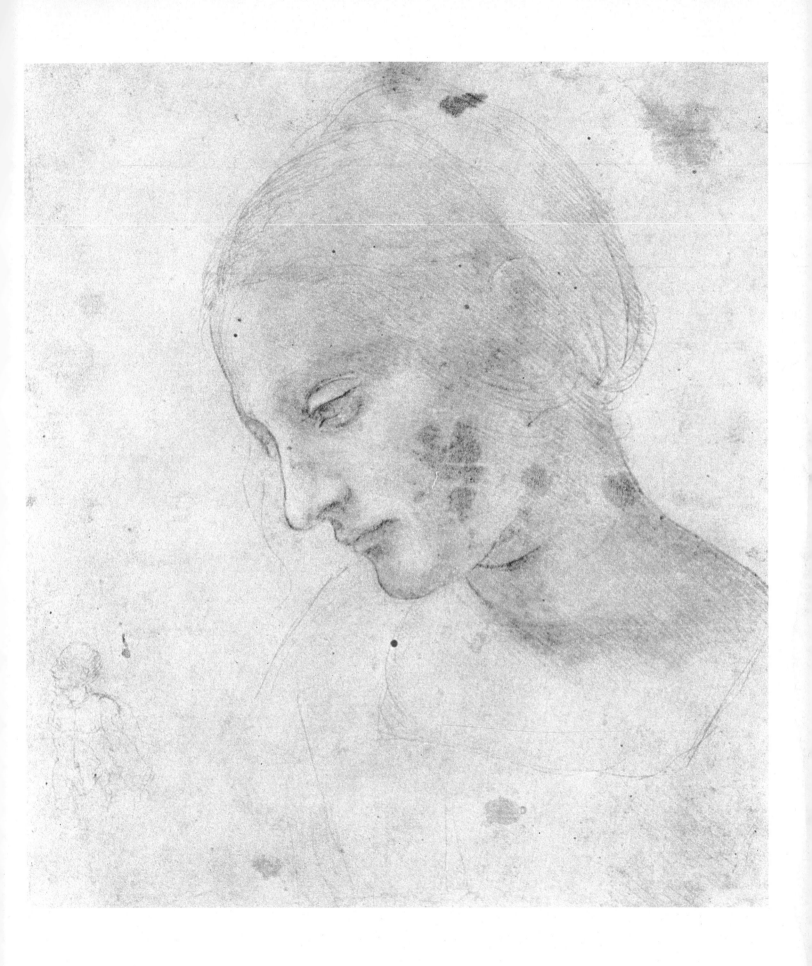

Plate 11 Study for Litta Madonna, 1480 or 1485, silverpoint on
prepared paper, 7⅛″ x 6⅝″, Louvre, Paris

Plate 12 Litta Madonna, 1480 or 1485, tempera on canvas,
16½″ x 13″, Hermitage, Leningrad

Plate 13 Adoration of the Magi, 1481-82, underpainting on panel,
8′ 1⅛″ x 7′ 11⅞″, Uffizi, Florence

Plate 14 Adoration of the Magi, detail - Virgin and Child

Plate 15 St. Jerome, c. 1483, underpainting on panel,
3′ 4⅝″ x 2′ 5½″, Vatican Museum, Rome

Plate 16 The Lady with the Ermine, c. 1483-86, oil on panel,
21¾″ x 15⅞″, Czartoryski Museum, Cracow

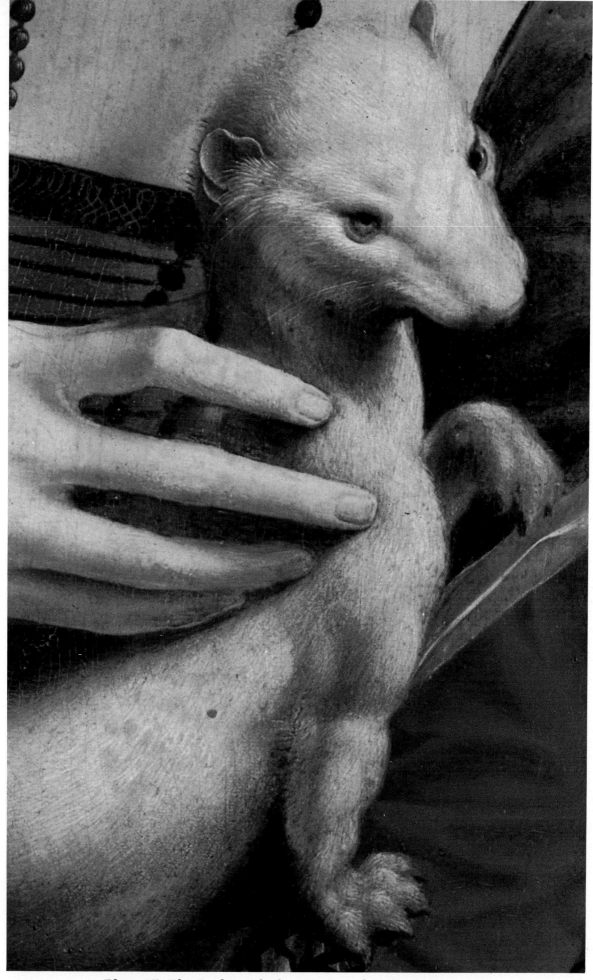

Plate 17 The Lady with the Ermine, detail - the ermine 33

Plate 18 Madonna of the Rocks, 1483-85, oil on panel,
6′ 3″ x 3′ 7½″, Louvre, Paris

Plate 19 Madonna of the Rocks, detail - head of Madonna

Plate 20 Portrait of a Woman, c. 1490, oil on panel,
20⅛″ x 13¾″, Biblioteca Ambrosiana, Milan

Plate 21 La Belle Ferronnière, c. 1490, oil on panel.
2′ ½″ x 17⅜″, Louvre, Paris

Plate 22 Girl with Bonnet, c. 1493-95, silverpoint on paper,
12½″ x 7⅝″, Royal Library, Windsor

Plate 23 Attributed to Leonardo, **The Savior**, c. 1495, pastel on
paper - restored, 15¾″ x 12½″, Brera Museum, Milan   39

Plate 24 Last Supper, c. 1495-98, oil tempera mixture on wall,
14′ x 30′, refectory of Sta Maria delle Grazie, Milan

Plate 25 Last Supper, detail - Christ

42   **Plate 26 Last Supper,** detail - Judas, John, and Peter

Plate 27 Last Supper, detail - Thomas, James the Greater, and Phillip   43

44   **Plate 28 Last Supper,** detail - Bartholomew, James the Lesser, and Andrew

Plate 29 Last Supper, detail - Matthew, Thaddeus, and Simon 45

Plate 30 Burlington House Cartoon, c. 1499-1501, charcoal with white
on brown paper, 4′ 7″ x 3′ 3⅞″, National Gallery, London

46

Plate 31 Burlington House Cartoon, detail - Infant and St. John   47

Plate 32 Burlington House Cartoon, detail - St. Anne

Plate 33 Burlington House Cartoon, detail - the Virgin

Plate 34 St. Anne, c. 1501, sanguine, black, and white chalk on red
prepared paper, 9¾″ x 7⅜″, Royal Library, Windsor

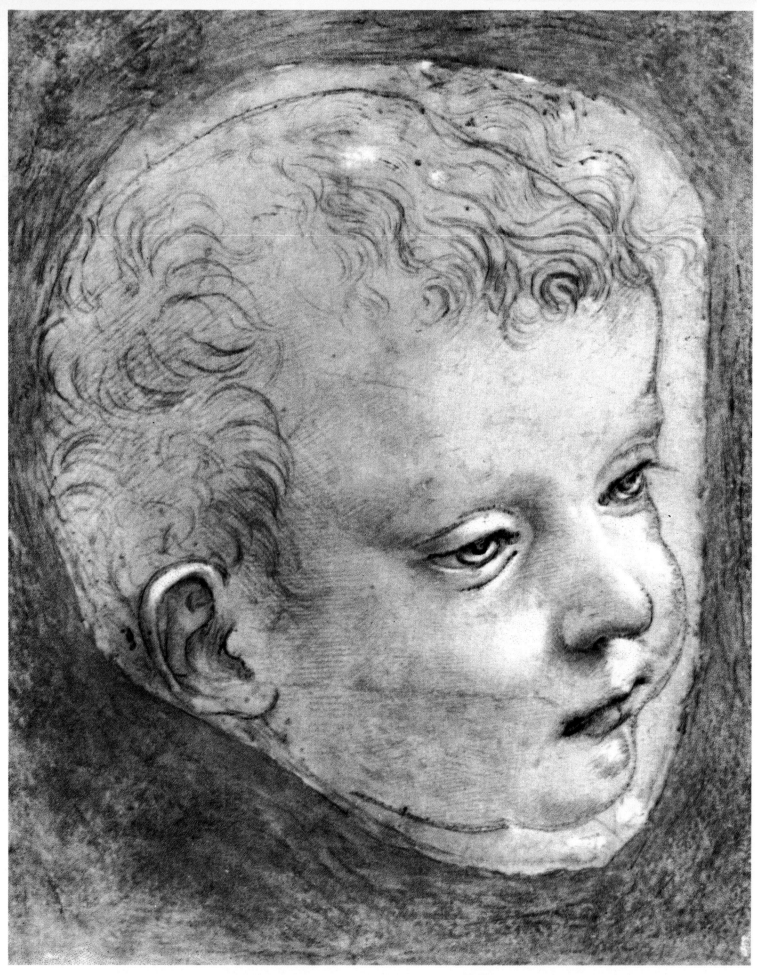

Plate 35 Head of Infant Turned to the Right, c. 1499-1501, pen and silverpoint
with white highlights on gray prepared paper, 6¾" x 5½", Louvre, Paris   51

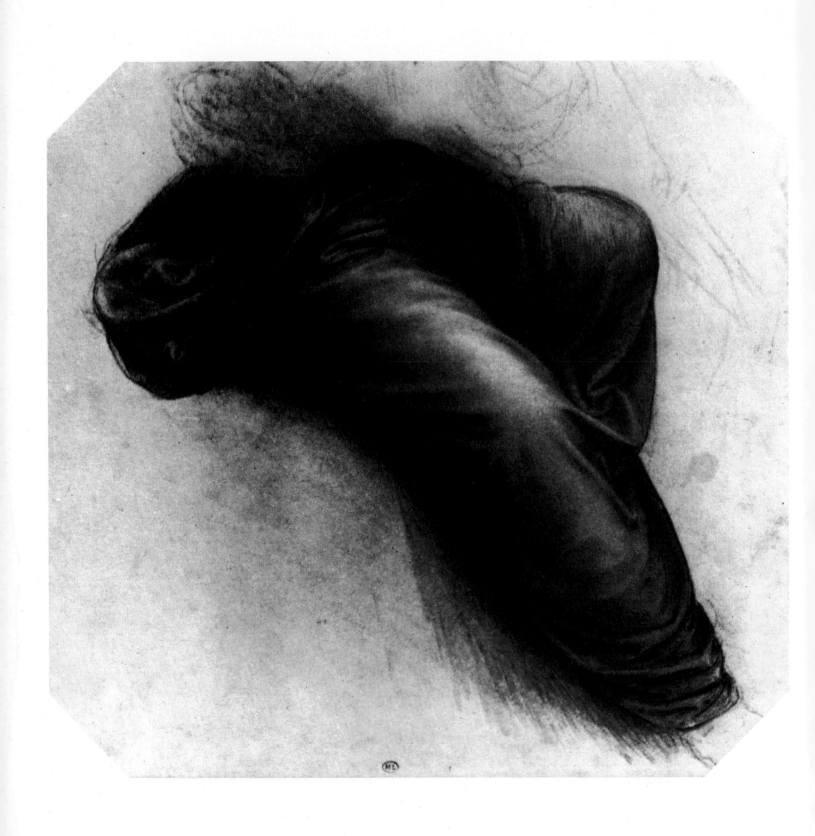

Plate 36 Study of Drapery, c. 1499-1501, drawing in brush on linen,
7⅜″ x 9¼″, Louvre, Paris

Plate 37 Isabella d'Este, 1500, black chalk, sanguine, and
pastel on paper, 24⅞″ x 18⅛″ , Louvre, Paris   53

54   **Plate 38 Mona Lisa,** 1503-08, oil on panel, 30¼″ x 20⅞″, Louvre, Paris

Plate 39 Mona Lisa, detail - her hands

Plate 40 Portrait of a Young Lady, attributed to Leonardo's studio,
early 16th century, oil on panel, 18½″ x 13⅜″,
National Gallery of Art, Washington, D. C.

Plate 41 Madonna of the Rocks, 1506-08, oil on panel,
6′ x 2⅝″ x 3′ 11¼″, National Gallery, London

Plate 42 Madonna of the Rocks, detail - the angel

Plate 43 Study for Leda, c. 1510, drawing in pen on paper,
Chateau Sforza, Milan

Plate 44 Virgin and Child with St. Anne, c. 1508-10,
oil on panel, 5′ 6⅜″ x 4′ 3¼″, Louvre, Paris

Plate 45 Virgin and Child with St. Anne, detail - St. Anne's head   61

Plate 46 St. John the Baptist, c. 1509-12, oil on panel,
27¼″ x 22½″, Louvre, Paris

Plate 47 Bacchus, 1511-15, oil on canvas, 5′ 9¾″ x 3′ 9¼″, Louvre, Paris   63

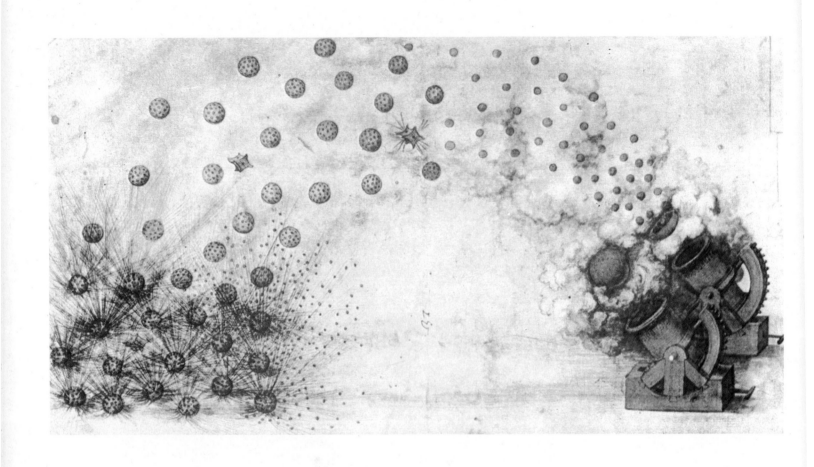

Plate 48 Explosive Bombardment, notebook drawing, Codex Atlantico, Folio 9, verso A, Biblioteca Ambrosiana, Milan